How To (& Retain) The Right Staff

By

Graham Martin

The Recruitment Guy

Published by Graham Martin

Publishing partner: Paragon Publishing, Rothersthorpe

First published 2013

ISBN 978-1-78222-040-4

Book design, layout and production management by Into Print

www.intoprint.net

01604 832149

Printed and bound in UK and USA by Lightning Source

For my dear Mum, Joyce Martin,
Thank you for everything

this book will help you...

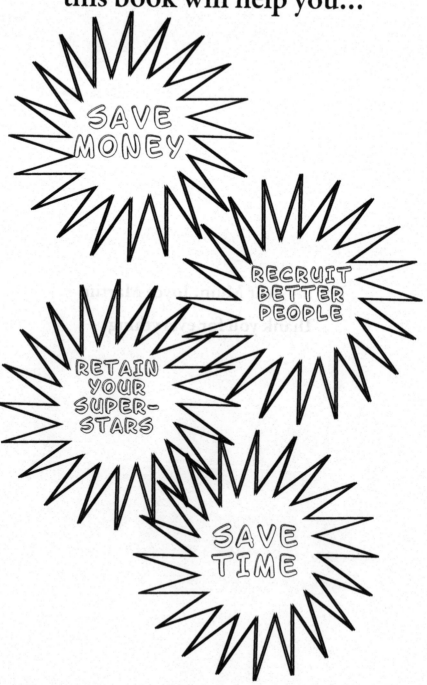

Contents

Foreword   6

Introduction – Before You Start   8

Chapter One – Stop...Wait A Minute!   10

Chapter Two – Job descriptions & Person Specifications   12

Chapter Three – Sources of Candidates   20

Chapter Four – Recruitment Agents ...Villains or Heroes?   28

Chapter Five – Getting The Best From *Your* Recruitment Agency   46

Chapter Six – Advertising   49

Chapter Seven – Vital Pre-Interview Activities   60

Chapter Eight – The Interview Process   64

Chapter Nine – Skills Testing & Personality Profiling   67

Chapter Ten – Making The Offer   70

Chapter Eleven – Contracts of Employment   72

Chapter Twelve – Post Acceptance Strategy   74

Chapter Thirteen – Protecting Your Investment   76

Chapter Fourteen – Commencement and Induction   77

Chapter Fifteen – Retaining Talent   78

Conclusions   81

What They Say...   81

Acknowledgements   82

The Author   83

Foreword

After nearly twenty five years recruiting for a huge number of businesses across a wide spectrum of sectors. I have personally helped hundreds of companies recruit thousands of staff covering many disciplines. During this time I have seen how poor preparation and follow up have meant that many deserving companies have been unable to hire suitable staff, or who, perhaps, even worse have failed to hang onto them once they have actually started!

Similarly, I have worked with many organisations who have helped fund my pension pot needlessly! Why? Not because I failed to recruit exceptional staff for them, but because they were, and often still are, dreadful at staff retention. Their lack of respect for their personnel is breathtaking; no induction, no appraisals, no training etc etc. Do I still recruit for them? No, but other agents will but willingly collude with them in a genuine waste of 'human resource'. I believe that 'good' recruiters have a duty of care to look after those coming to us for support in their job search. Changing jobs is a 'big deal', it's 'up there' with moving home, having children and choosing a life partner. I and many in my profession (yes, many of us do belong to accrediting bodies that assess our standards) enjoy getting it 'right', sourcing an outstanding candidate for a genuine organisation and seeing both parties benefit.

This book is designed for the non-HR manager who has responsibility for the recruitment process although HR professionals may also find it useful as a refresher, a source of new ideas or as a guide to help them recruit better staff, more effectively, and get the best out of their relationship with recruitment agencies.

If you are reading this book, I assume that you have either total or joint responsibility for the recruitment process and associated budgetary issues. Whilst many of the strategies discussed in this book do also apply to the public sector, there is no doubt that bureaucracy and, in my opinion, needless political correctness often mean that a different methodology and philosophical approach is required. This book is, therefore aimed primarily at the private sector and at SME businesses in particular.

For the sake of simplicity, whenever I refer to 'him', I may also be alluding to 'her'. Likewise, 'he' could mean 'she'.

Introduction

Before You Start

It happens every day, but especially on Mondays! A knock on the door, or the request for a "quick word". There they stand, shuffling from foot to foot with a white envelope in their hand .....you know what's coming "Sorry, but I'm leaving". Your reactions could include; despair...this person is simply irreplaceable; anger...how much time has it taken you to train this person? Betrayal...this was your protégé, don't they realise how much you had to fight for their promotion! Or maybe, you're relieved; they were useless and they've done you a real favour!

The reaction of many employers is to dig out the job specification of the person due to leave, put an advert in the local paper or the internet and wait for the phone to ring or their email box to fill up!

Alternatively, you decide you need to recruit an additional member of staff rather than a replacement. Again, many employers will simply place an advert and wait for responses to flood in.

It never ceases to amaze me how many employers spend more time and effort thinking about the purchase of a new company car or computer than they do considering the many issues relating to a new member of staff. Sure, the lease of a new company car may cost £5,000 per year. With insurance, petrol and maintenance, the costs could well double....but these pale into insignificance compared to the costs associated with hiring staff.

Assuming an annual salary of £20,000. With National Insurance Contributions, holiday cover and an on-going provision for training; you're looking at the thick end of £30,000! Indeed, assuming an average tenure of 4 years, the recruitment of such staff equates to an investment of approx £120,000! And yet, many organisations still devote little effort in ensuring they hire the right people first time round. Heads may well roll if the wrong car or computer system is bought; but what damage will be caused by hiring the wrong member of staff? The recruitment process itself is costly enough; time and money spent advertising, developing job descriptions, sifting through reams of applications, contacting candidates, setting up and conducting interviews, issuing offer letters and rejections, induction courses etc, etc. Of course, using recruitment agency services will reduce much of the time and effort spent on hiring staff, but if things go wrong, you could have spent between 10% and 30% of the new employee's salary with little or nothing to show for it! Ouch!!

Simply spending time considering the type of person required, how to recruit and hang on to them will pay massive dividends. Imagine asking a builder to build you a "nice family home"! He'll say "Great, show me the plans" and "What's the budget?" You wouldn't dream of saying "Well, I don't have any plans....but I know you're a great builder; just build me what you think". What a disaster! So why should recruiting staff be treated any less seriously?

The next chapters will take you through a step-by-step process to ensure you reduce the risk of disaster to a bare minimum.

Note: As the owner of a recruitment agency myself, I am biased! I believe that the recruitment sector has a great deal to offer and can make a huge contribution to businesses of all types. Personally, I have found it an honour to work with hundreds of enlightened, outstanding employers over the past 25 years and indeed have had the privilege of interviewing thousands of people and placing nearly 2000 candidates in permanent work. My business has also placed many thousands of people in temporary work in hundreds of companies.

I do, however, recognise that many organisations prefer, for many reasons, to carry out some, if not all aspects of the recruitment process in-house. This book, therefore, is designed, for the most part, for those wishing to "Do It Yourself". For those, perhaps more "enlightened" employers who do use recruitment agencies (see, I told you I was biased), this book will help you get better levels of service from your recruiters, better value for money and reduce the risk if things do go wrong.

Chapter One

Stop...Wait A Minute!

Before you start to recruit, what are you looking for? Your credit controller, (let's call her Debbie) has just resigned and you need a replacement. You need another Debbie, right? Well not necessarily. Of course Debbie's departure will leave a gaping hole in your business (and let's face it, debt collection and cash flow are vital to any organisation) but it does not always follow that you need to replace like for like.

Whilst the job function may remain broadly the same, your organisation or specific department in question may have evolved since you last recruited. The average period of employment in the UK is thirty months. If a week is a long time in politics, it is even longer in modern day business. Thirty months is an age, and so much will have changed.

Now is the perfect time to reconsider the demands of the role. Please don't be tempted to simply dust off the job description (if indeed you have one) that you used last time and instruct the individual responsible for recruitment to "find me another one of these".

Let's consider the credit control scenario again. The main responsibility may well be to chase outstanding debts, but it may well be appropriate to incorporate other duties into the role. For example, credit control may take less time than it used to because the number of clients has reduced, perhaps the additional time available could be used carrying out sales ledger maintenance duties or even sales invoicing. Alternatively, maybe the sales ledger has grown due to expansion or a wider number of clients. Maybe this is an ideal opportunity to reinforce the function by hiring a senior credit controller who would be more experienced than Debbie.

The permutations are infinite. Every role in every organisation will evolve as time passes. Do not ignore this excellent opportunity to restructure the way your organisation operates. Consider the telex operator that used to have a crucial role in many large operations...technology has moved on and those people either retrained or are wondering what happened to their careers. Whatever happened to the typing pool, the tea lady and legions of clerks in insurance company head offices? Technology, that's what! Whilst these may well be obvious examples, the truth is that many roles do not disappear, they just evolve. Here I am, typing this book on my PC at work (slowly I might add). Ten years ago, my assistant would have transcribed this from my audio machine, or I might have dictated it to a shorthand typist. Until the last recession kicked in, I had an assistant but she was less of a secretary and more of an administrator or PA. The role of the assistant has evolved; the title may remain but the duties and demands have changed. Over time, almost every position from office junior to chairman has evolved.

Also consider the people issues; building effective teams is not the easiest of management tasks, but one of the most important. There are many exceptional books that cover this issue specifically, but briefly, consider the personalities within the department right now. Did Debbie "fit in", if not why not? If she didn't, was it because her personality did not match that of her colleagues? Having said this, remember that diversity is essential to a balanced community. If everyone was an introvert or the life and soul of the party, the organisation would be unbalanced.

Chapter Two

Job Descriptions & Person Specifications

Irrespective of whether you are intending to recruit your new employee through the internet, a newspaper advert, word of mouth or recruitment organisation, it is vital that you create a detailed job description and personal specification (JD/PS). This document can be used as a blueprint. Those that are "in the loop" concerning this position should have some input, and whilst I would not suggest that any job description and personal specification be the collective work of a committee, (I have seen these and they tend for the most part to be pages of compromise) it is useful to get the input of others. Ultimately, however, one person must have the final responsibility for this document. I would suggest that the individual who has this responsibility is also the person to whom the new employee will report. In the case of the relatively junior manager who is to have somebody under his wing for the first time, there is a good chance that he will not have had the opportunity of developing a JD/PS before and will need to be coached.

Similarly it is important that the manager who has responsibility/ ownership of this document and to whom the new member of staff will directly report, will have had at least some input into the decision of whom to hire. I have seen many campaigns fail dramatically when an excellent new employee is "dumped on" an unsuspecting manager who then goes out of his way to jeopardise the success of this new member of staff. Whilst I fully appreciate that many larger companies employ HR professionals to co-ordinate the recruitment process, or perhaps the trusted PA of the managing director has historically placed adverts and carried out initial interviews, it is crucial that those at the sharp end have input into the creation of an up to date JD and that the new employee's direct boss at least feels that they have been involved in the decision making process. Nobody likes to feel that they have had somebody foisted upon them and indeed coaching a junior manager in this essential aspect of business will mean that they become increasingly more effective. And, if you buy into the philosophy behind Investors In People, such empowerment makes sense.

So, without devoting a whole book to this essential process, here are some guidelines:-

- Keep thing simple and endeavour to keep it to less than two pages of typed A4.

- Wherever possible use the previous JD as a starting point. There is no need to reinvent the wheel after all.

- Discuss the specifics of the role with existing/outgoing individuals who carry out this function. As either a director or line manager, the person who develops this JD will probably not be quite as conversant as to the specific duties involved and the proportion of time spent on that particular duty as someone who has/is actually doing the job themselves.

- Use this as an opportunity to re-consider how this role has evolved since you last recruited for it. Things change, ensure that you address developments such as the economy, technology, client needs, products etc.

- Create or update a list of the duties involved, the amount of time spent fulfilling them and their importance.

There are thousands of job titles that I could consider in creating a generic blueprint and of course one size will not fit all, however, these are the headings that I suggest you consider when developing your own JD.

- **Company profile.** Remembering that this document should be used not only for internal consumption but should also be provided to recruitment organisations that you have engaged or will be sent to prospective candidates prior to interview, it is appropriate to write a few short paragraphs about what your organisation does, for whom, ethos, culture, ownership and plans for the future.

- **Department.** Just a few lines on the number of staff in this particular department, its staffing levels, reporting structure and how it fits in to the business.

- **Overall objectives.** What are the main (no more than three at the most) objectives of this job?

- **Duties.** Avoiding techno-babble or industry specific jargon, list the duties providing, where possible, levels of priority and an idea of how much time spent.

- **Resources controlled.** If this person will have other staff or departments reporting into them, explain what they are.

- **Equipment used.** Whether it be a JCB digger, an Apple Mac computer or state of the art medical diagnostic equipment, it is important that this be recorded. Candidates will be keen to know what they will be using.

- **Locations.** Will the employee work purely at one location or will they travel to other sites. If so, where, when and how often.

- **Prospects.** What opportunities are there for progression within this role? How would someone be able to progress?

- **Training.** What, if any, training will be provided, by whom and how often. Are there any qualifying issues such as passing probation, previous qualifications or the requirement for the new employee to study outside of work or contribute towards the training?

- **Money.** How much is offered from day one and how could the successful candidate earn more over a period of time?

The next aspect of this vital document is the person specification (PS). With so much written about sexual discrimination and equal opportunities elsewhere I am sure that I do not have to expound the virtues of a balanced view to recruiting the appropriate staff, irrespective of colour, creed or race. Whilst companies are often used to thinking about the job description, they rarely spend much time thinking about the personal specification. The result of this is that many companies recruit people with the *skills* to carry out the role, but who for any number of reasons leave within a relatively short period of time (or who are pushed out) just because they didn't fit in. A recent survey stated that only 9% of Londoners had their "dream job". Much of this responsibility has to be laid at the feet of the employers who either misrepresent the role or who hire square pegs for round holes. Let's consider therefore, some aspects that might help us identify a suitable candidate.

- **Age.** This is a hot potato due to legislation that ensures that we do not discriminate about age. I am certainly against ageism, however, I believe it foolish not to consider how a new employee may fit in with the existing team. Imagine a department of, say, "fifty something" credit controllers. Whilst I am not suggesting that you proactively state that you will only consider applications from those of a similar age group, it is only fair that you highlight that the team is *currently* made up of such a demographic age group since some (but not all) youngsters may prefer to work with those of a similar age. On the other hand, I know of some teenagers who have wanted to work with those closer to their grandparents' age because they wish to avoid potential backbiting over dress sense and felt that they could learn more from those with decades of work experience. Do not be restrictive, simply advise applicants of the current situation and let them make up their own mind.

- **Skills and experience required.** It is vital that you establish and communicate the appropriate levels of competence for any particular role since there are positions that require a reduced or greater level of experience. This could cover any number of the thousands of careers and jobs that are on offer today. Avoid overestimating the requirement for a candidate to have a specific level of competence. For example are you really looking for a typist that has a speed of 60 words per minute, when in reality your outgoing employee is significantly slower, but more importantly, is accurate! I have often been told by employers that they require advanced levels of IT skills, but when questioning further have found that the job really only demands a basic understanding or at most intermediate. To determine what is required may demand some research. However, this may be done without too much difficulty by benchmarking existing staff's skill levels via one of the many internet based online IT skills assessment services. Alternatively, colleges and training organisations may be able to provide this for you, either in house or externally, for minimal cost. Recruitment agencies will often do this as part of their service.

- **Achievements and Qualifications.** In addition to the above, what specific qualifications are needed, *not* just preferred? I have lost count of the number of times that I have spoken to companies demanding a degree or a specific accountancy qualification, for example, only to have them reconsider this requirement when it is pointed out that a degree does not necessarily mean that the candidate has the mental faculties or experience required. Similarly, just because a person did *not* obtain a degree does not mean that they are not intelligent or cannot make a contribution to an organisation. I know several millionaires personally, only one of who has a degree! And, no, I am not referring to illiterate Rolls Royce owning scrap metal merchants or rock musicians. I refer to articulate, well-informed, hard working professionals who *chose* to go out to work at 16 or 18 rather than pursue further education.

- **Location and Transport.** As discussed previously, what is your preferred catchment area? How far is it reasonable to expect an employee to travel? Is it vital that they have their own transport because there are no buses for example? If a company vehicle is provided are there any insurance restrictions relating to age, years' experience or a limit to the number or seriousness of driving offences they have on their licence.

- **Personality and Communication Skills.** Are you looking for someone who will deal with strangers on a first time basis and will therefore need to be fairly confident or will they be fairly isolated? Will this person be in a situation, such as a hotel front of house position where they will need to be very well spoken? Will they need a great deal of patience because they will be dealing with 'difficult' staff members or clients?

- **Personal Presentation.** If you require someone to be very well presented, possibly because they will have contact with the public or clients, then say so. On the other hand, I have one client in particular (a firm of architects) who proactively encourage a slightly more trendy image. When I found them a beautifully spoken receptionist who had several dozen facial piercings, they were thrilled! Do not assume that every one thinks that 'smartly dressed' means the same thing. Explain what you mean!

- **Flexibility.** How often (if at all) will the new employee be expected to start early or stay late? Are weekends ever worked (maybe for annual stock check)? Is it a requirement of the role that the employee attend overseas meetings or client entertainment events? Will their partner/spouse be invited?

In addition to the job description and person specification, what other elements are worth noting? Many aspects may already be covered in your company handbook or contract of employment, however the following, whilst not exhaustive, is reasonably comprehensive and should be included in any contract of employment.

- **Salary.** As discussed earlier, ensure that you are paying the market rate. It is worth quoting a salary band since you may be prepared to pay slightly more for a credit controller with experience of your client profile than a more generic credit controller with no industry experience. I would suggest that you state a range of no more than 10%. With public sector or larger private sector organisations, a specific salary or grading system may be relevant. When are salaries reviewed and upon what basis? Is a salary increased purely upon merit or is a % increase used; maybe based upon government inflation figures.

- **Probation.** Rather than confirm permanent employment from day one, it is totally appropriate to put a probationary clause into any contract of employment. Whether this period be one, three or six months depends primarily upon the seniority of the role and how long is reasonable for a new employee in that position to prove themselves.

- **Appraisals.** Following best practice means providing regular appraisals. These may be monthly, quarterly or annually and should be taken seriously, prepared for and documented. There are many excellent management books explaining in detail the different types of appraisal; the only recommendations I have is that firstly you actually commit to the concept of appraisal and secondly that you are prepared for the process to evolve. In my experience, the best appraisal systems are bespoke to a company and have developed over a period of time.

- **Reviews.** It is important to carry out (and stick to) a regular review schedule. A review may (or may not) be connected to an appraisal process. A review does **not,** however, necessarily imply an increase in salary; simply the *opportunity* to discuss matters.

- **Hours.** What are the official hours and is there a difference between them and what is actually required to carry out the role? For example, a management role may have official hours of 9am to 5-30pm, but may have a clause requiring him to work "whatever hours are needed to carry out the demands of the job". Is overtime paid or time off in lieu offered? Do you limit the hours worked under the 48-hour average/17 week Working Time Directive or do you require your staff to opt out?

- **Holidays.** How many days are provided? Are any required for statutory closedowns (such as at Christmas)? Do the number of days increase with service? And to how many as a maximum? Can staff carry days forward to the next year?

- **Sick, Maternity and Paternity Pay.** Do you offer the statutory or more?

- **Unions.** Is there one or more union operating at your organisation or do you state that you do not recognise membership?

- **Commissions and Bonuses.** What criteria are used? This is particularly important in the case of sales positions or executive appointments which are rewarded upon stock market performance or profitability, for example.

- **Share options.** Describe these in detail or refer to a separate document as provided by your accountants or lawyers.

- **Company cars and allowances.** If a vehicle is provided, is there a choice? What responsibility for the vehicle does the employee have? Is there a cash alternative?

- **Pension scheme.** What is on offer, is there a qualifying period? Is it part or contributory?

- **Private Health.** As above, what do you cover and what qualifying period is there? Is it fully funded?

- **Life Insurance.** Many organisations offer such insurance to a surviving spouse/partner or family member based upon a multiplier of salary.

- **Canteen, tea making, vending etc.** What do you offer and is it subsidised? If so is it treated as a benefit in kind and therefore treated as taxable income?

- **Sports Club Facilities or gym membership.** Whether it is an in-house facility or membership to a public facility or private club, is it free and if so is it a benefit in kind as above?

- **Confidentiality.** Will you require the new employee to sign such a clause?

- **Notice period.** What is required? Does it change after a period, such as after probation?

- **Internet & Email Policy.** The new 'hot potato'. I strongly suggest that you don't ignore this but take professional advice on how to deal with social media and email/web related issues at work.

Chapter Three

Sources of Candidates

So, you've worked out exactly what you are trying to achieve by recruiting for a particular position and you have developed a complete Job Description and Person Specification. All you have to do now is find your ideal candidate. But from where? The alternatives open to today's manager are many. I have summarised the pros and cons and comments for all the major options:-

Advertising in The Local Newspaper

Pros

- Easy to organise

- Weekly publications mean that your advert could appear that week

- Very cost effective if successful

- Builds awareness of your organisation in local community

Cons

- You need to write the advert yourself

- No guarantee of any results

- Your money will be wasted if the advert is not successful

- Indiscreet; your competition will always know what positions you are hiring for unless you use PO Box numbers. Many candidates prefer *not* to apply to such anonymous adverts as they fear that they *may* be applying to their *existing* employer

- Lack of confidentiality; especially if you are trying to replace an existing member of staff!

- Time consuming; you have to deal with each response yourself

- Too slow; by the time you have sent out an application form and agreed to interview a short-list, your 'ideal' candidate may have found employment elsewhere

- Frustrating; you arrange an interview, only for the candidate not to turn up or be delayed because they got lost

- Annoying; you interview a candidate who looked great on paper, only to realise that they are clearly unsuitable

- Lengthy; at least half of your interview time will be taken up briefing the candidate about the role and the company

- Could well get more calls from recruitment agencies 'selling their wares' than real live candidates!

Advertising In Specialist or Trade Press

Pros
- Read by a limited audience, specific to a particular industry or profession

- Rarely cheap, but can still be good value if successful

- Builds awareness of your organisation's brand within your industry

Cons
- Can be expensive as there may only be a few specialist trade publications to chose from and they may well have the monopoly

- Printing deadlines may mean that you have just missed the 'cut off date' and you have to wait six weeks until your advert is seen by the target audience

- As above, consider speed, confidentiality and frustration.

Generalist Internet Job Sites

Pros
- Limited cost (some are free!)

- Potentially huge audience

- Easy to use

- Candidates may apply the day you 'post' the vacancy onto the internet

Cons

- As for advertising in papers but also:-

- Candidates apply from outside your geographical area and this can be very frustrating

- Need to keep checking your email account every few hours

Specialist and Industry Specific Job Sites

Pros

- Specific audience

- Immediate impact

- Easy to use

Cons

- Again, as for advertising in newspapers and generic websites but can be rather expensive.

- Many of these so-called "specialist" websites are poorly promoted and do not generate decent results. It is important to ask for testimonial evidence from previous users. Ask for a 24-hour free trial if you are not sure. If they are confident, they should at least be prepared to offer some incentive.

CV Databases

There are many commercial CV databases that provide access to a large number of "allegedly" current job seekers. Some are stand-alone, others are linked to job sites. I have experienced both excellent and dismal results by using these databases. Specialist, industry specific, databases may only have a limited number of CVs registered whilst the larger better known sites may have 100,000's of less specialised job seekers. My recommendation is that you try them; but only on a free trial or limited cost basis. The CVs on many (but *not* all of these databases) are out of date. I have emailed so many allegedly "hot candidates" only for them to email me back saying that they had found another position a year before. The key is enquire as to how often the database is cleansed and, for example, how many CVs were posted within, say, the last two months?

Your Own Website

This is a 'no-brainer' really. It will cost you next to nothing to advertise your own vacancies on your website. You never know, you may get lucky; especially if you get a large volume of traffic to your site. It is worth considering developing your 'web site marketing strategy' so that if someone uses Google or other search engines to identify "jobs at ABC Ltd" that your appropriate web page will feature high in the rankings. This should not be used as the sole methodology to attract candidates however.

Word Of Mouth

Again, easy to do, but you'd be amazed how few people really make this work for them. Think about the number of people that you know via business, children's clubs, church, trade associations, parent teacher associations, school, sports teams etc. Whilst you don't want to be known as an individual who only discusses their company's staffing needs at a social, sports or church gathering, it is easy to mention your employment requirements during casual conversation. For example "so, how's business?" It's a casual enquiry, often offered between business people. Rather than saying "yes, fine thanks" how about saying " great, but I'm really struggling to recruit a sales person/accountant/etc, etc" This simple comment will, on occasion, produce results. Whilst the person you are talking with may not necessarily be interested themselves, they may have a friend, relative or current work colleague who could be suitable. Your comment may not produce results immediately, but by sowing such seeds, you are likely to get a call out of the blue every now and then. "Graham, it's Dan from the tennis club here. Last week you mentioned that you are looking for a credit controller. Well a friend of my wife has just been made redundant/ has just moved into the area/etc and is looking for a position in credit control. Shall I give her your number/ do you want to call her?".

Just remember to say "thank you" to your contact if this strategy produces results. They will have done you a *huge* favour and probably saved you hundreds if not thousands of pounds. They may well be a source of other candidates too; so nurture them. You don't need to shower them with money (they may even be offended) but a 'thank you' card, a bottle of champagne or bouquet of flowers may be sufficient. Alternatively, perhaps a voucher for a meal for two might be suitable.

Financial Incentives

As opposed to the casual, "by the way" approach above, many companies run formal introduction incentive schemes for their own staff. Who knows your organisation better than your own staff and who better to 'sell' your organisation's employment opportunities than these staff? (This *could* backfire of course if you are *not* a great manager *or* if the company has a poor reputation for staff welfare and pay!). Assuming your organisation does not struggle with such problems; it should be easy to introduce an effective referral scheme.

Simply inform *every* member of staff about *every* role that is available (and not commercially sensitive of course) and offer them a tangible reward for recommending someone to you. Such a reward could be cash, vouchers, extra days holiday etc. Remember that, as above, such a referral will have saved the company not only money but time and is well worth rewarding. Two points of caution however! There should be a qualifying period before payment is made to limit your expense should the person leave within, say, three months. Secondly, remember that incentives are often deemed 'benefits in kind' and are subject to taxation. I suggest that you discuss tangible incentives with your accountant or auditors before finalising the details of any scheme.

Social Networking

Facebook, Google+, Twitter and Linkedin are not the only social networking sites worth mentioning but they are, as of writing, probably the best known of their genre although, as of writing, Google+ is gaining momentum. There is no doubt in my opinion, that they are an incredibly powerful method of communicating about an opportunity to a wide audience. This is not the place to explain how to use these tools to attract candidates. Simply searching the web using phrases such as 'how to use FaceBook/Twitter/Linkedin to recruit staff' will provide a deluge of information. I find that having teenage children also helps with any technical aspects of the medium!

Pros

- Cheap, fast **and** easy to use

Cons

- Not confidential, difficult to 'switch off' the post once it's gone 'live'

Recruitment Agencies

Pros

- Usually "no results, no fee"

- Candidates often available immediately for interview from existing database

- Some candidates available on a temporary basis for you to 'try before you buy'

- Some agencies will make direct approaches to candidates who are not currently on any database or who respond to adverts. If an agency manages to attract such a candidate on your behalf, you will invariably recruit someone who you do not have to compete with against any other employer.

- Confidential and discreet

- Candidates should have been skills assessed before interview

- Many recruitment organisations will take references upon a candidate *but* I would always urge you to take up your own

- The recruitment organisation in question *should* brief each candidate before the interview with you so that you don't have to spend valuable time explaining exactly what your company does and the specifics of the role

- Some recruitment organisations will offer the opportunity to interview at their own offices. This provides you with a distraction free zone!

- Free replacement guarantees and financial rebates are often offered if things 'don't work out'

- Some recruitment organisations will deliver each candidate to your door, avoiding the 'lost applicant' scenario

- You are provided with feedback after the interview. How well did *you* come across? Does the candidate *want* to work for you?

- Declining the offer. The recruitment organisation will advise the unsuccessful candidates for you; hopefully in a manner that makes them still feel good about themselves and positive about your company.

- Salary negotiations. The recruitment organisation should be skilled at brokering a mutually acceptable deal and will know what the candidate is *really* looking for. This can be difficult if there is no intermediary.

- Maintaining contact. It is essential that the recruitment organisation keeps in contact with the candidate before the start date to ensure that they can quell any 'last minute nerves' or possibly intercept a counter offer by an existing employer. Additionally the recruitment organisation can provide you with feedback during the first month or so of your new member of staff's employment. Are they settling in well, are they having any problems? Are they struggling with the IT system and need more training?

I make NO excuse for my list of 'pros' regarding using agencies being so long; I am biased remember!

Cons

- Can be expensive if person leaves within a short period and no free replacement or only a meagre financial rebate offered

- Some recruitment organisations don't take the time to fully understand their clients' needs and as a result waste everyone's time by submitting candidates who are clearly unsuitable

- Time can also be wasted by the submission of several poor quality candidates to make an 'average' one appear even better

- Some, in my opinion, recruitment organisations lacking integrity, will use the opportunity to meet a prospective client, as a 'talent sourcing exercise'. Whilst you decide not to engage their services, they have found out who your key staff are, and they begin to approach them for roles with their existing clients. If you have no reason to believe that the recruitment organisation in question is anything other than 100% genuine, get them to sign a simple confidentiality agreement.

- As above, some 'less than scrupulous' recruiters will maintain contact with a candidate after they have placed him with a client company. They then place them elsewhere after a period of time has passed and collect a second fee! Sharp practice and highly dubious at best, totally unacceptable if you ask me. A simple clause should eradicate such an occurrence.

Chapter Four

Recruitment Agents...Villains or Heroes?

Like most business service companies, there are the exceptional, mediocre and dreadful! We all know better accountants than others and don't get me started on the legal profession! Recruitment agencies can be a fantastic ally in the search for exceptional staff, but they can, on occasion, be guilty of wasting clients' time by submitting unsuitable candidates because they have not understood the brief, have nobody available at that specific time or are simply incompetent! Depending upon your requirements, a relationship with the recruitment sector *can* be an efficient, cost effective method of sourcing the staff you require within the time frame you demand. Yes, going it alone may look like the cheaper option, but when weighed against the management time of placing advertisements, using on-line job sites, short-listing suitable candidates, arranging initial interviews, writing rejection letters, arranging second interviews, assessing candidates, taking initial references, making job offers and negotiating salaries and start dates, not to mention keeping in touch before their start date; recruitment agencies *can* offer great value for money.

So, what services do recruitment organisations provide?

Recruitment is a fast moving, innovative, entrepreneurial sector and there are many different services offered under its banner, depending upon specialisation. Below are a list of the services that *most* recruiters offer:-

- **Client visits.** By meeting the client at their premises, the recruiter will be able to establish details about the organisation that will not be evident simply by talking over the telephone; such as culture, environment, atmosphere etc.

- **Discuss the role.** As discussed previously, it is really important that you have drawn up the job description and person specification before you begin the recruitment process. However it is worth discussing this with a recruiter as they can often provide some essential input. They may have recommendations to make regarding the availability of the skills you require and the salary you believe the role should command. Are you offering too little....or too much? Can you *really* expect to recruit a credit controller with previous experience of collecting debts in Russia or should you expect to recruit an experienced credit controller that you can train further to carry out this vital function in your organisation!

- **Job Description and Person Specification.** If you have *not* previously prepared such a document, some recruitment organisations will offer to draft this for you.

- **Advertising.** Depending upon the type of recruitment organisation you have decided to work with, they may offer to pay for advertising themselves (whatever the media used) or they may request that you pay some or all of the cost. Many agencies will obtain a discount when advertising and *may* be prepared to pass this on to you. Alternatively, they may be prepared to design and place the advertisement, pass you the discount but charge a handling fee.

- **Response handling.** Dealing with recruitment advertising response, whether via Internet, newspaper or Social Media, is an important part of a successful campaign. Irrespective of the numbers of candidates that are generated by a campaign, fast response is crucial. The best candidates are, in any economy, in great demand. Unless an agency wants to lose an exceptional candidate to the competition and waste its investment in generating the candidate's interest it must be vigilant and be prepared to respond immediately to any interest.

- **Initial interviews.** For every 200 applications that my own recruitment agency generates, we only actually interview 10. This is because we are very choosy. Most agencies are! True, it might gain them a 'reputation' for poor customer service from the public in general but it is the employer who pays the agency, not the applicant. The vast majority of applications are irrelevant or from poorly qualified candidates. We don't want these people and neither do our clients. We throw them back into the 'sea'. Of the 10 that we do actually interview, we will probably only submit 3 for interview. Why? Simply, the initial interview highlights deficiencies in their experience or skills. Of the 3 that my own recruitment business submits to our clients, an average of 1 candidate will be offered a job! This is *not* an average ratio however. Most recruitment agencies only manage a 1 in 10 ratio!

- **Assessment of skills.** It is vital that an agency assess the skills of general office and more specialised candidates (such as accounts). Spelling, numeracy and IT assessments are vital. Most will do this for you but do ask for proof of test results. It is often possible to request that your agency customise the tests to suit your particular business or roles within a department. Just ask!

- **CV or not CV?** This is a bit of a puzzler! Do you ask for a CV or not? I have clients who insist on a CV before they will interview a candidate, others who simply want a set of bullet points with the CV to be provided before the interview. A few others HATE CVs and prefer applicants to complete their own application form; others...You get the idea! Every one has a different view of the CV. HR often need a CV or similar before their Director or manager will agree to interview someone! Decide what method YOU want to employ to decide to interview someone...and stick with it. Educate your recruiters and ensure they know what you expect from them. Remember to brief them fully and allow them to visit with you or ask you a great number of questions. Investing this time will pay dividends down the road. My clients accept my 'word' most of the time as long as I send the CV before the interview. After all, many of my candidates are sourced without a CV; to wait for a CV will occasionally mean that you lose out. Who REALLY misses out? We all do, the candidate, the recruiter and especially the employer!

- **References.** Most recruiters will state in their terms of business that they will NOT take references up on a candidate; although in practice many agencies will endeavour to obtain some kind of confirmation that the candidate is who they say they are and has the relevant experience they have said they have. The reason that most agencies do not commit to taking formal references is that in their terms of business, they state that it is the employers' responsibility to check suitability and references. This 'get out clause' is there for a reason of course. It indemnifies the recruitment firm against any loss incurred, should the candidate they put forward not be suitable. This is, in my humble opinion, fair enough. The agency is an 'introducer' of mutually willing parties, it is the responsibility of each party to assess their suitability. However, it is always a great idea to ask the agency what research they *have* done concerning 'your' candidate. We often take up verbal references from previous employers; it is amazing how much more information we find out over the phone than in writing. Yes, there is a whole debate about human rights, data protection etc that we could go into. But we won't! The rule is, just ask your recruiter how much research they have done regarding 'your' candidate.

- **Client briefing.** So, after you have decided what you want from your agency in terms of information, make sure you understand the candidates' motivators. Why are they moving, how much money do they want, what prospects do they seek? It is vital that the agency briefs you fully concerning the candidates' ambitions. No two candidates want the same thing remember! Training, prospects, security, variety etc. Only once you know what they want can you tailor your interview to suit each candidate.

- **Candidate briefing.** Your agency must brief your candidate fully prior to interview. They should provide the interviewee with a full job description, ideally approved by you and a synopsis of what will be expected of them at interview. I strongly urge that you check EXACTLY how your agency will prepare your candidate before the initial interview.

- **Feedback.** Feedback is vital- for all parties. Candidates CRAVE feedback, so please let the agency know how things went within 24 hours. More than 24 hours is, frankly rude....even if it's a 'no', just say so! And fast! Importantly, if you ARE interested in a candidate, explain why and explain the next steps. Keep people interested in the role and the organisation. Too often clients have missed out on great candidates because they have delayed providing a response, only for the candidate to accept a LOWER offer but from a more interested party! And in return, you need feedback from your agency; how was the interview for the candidate? Do they have any comments? Are they actually interested? Learn from this vital information...even if it hurts to hear it!

- **Rejection.** Ugh! It's an ugly word, isn't it? But I'm afraid that it's all part of the hiring process. Candidates that are not successful need to be advised accordingly. This is your agency's responsibility. But make sure that they do it with a sense of humanity. Check that they have understood why you have declined to hire them. Give constructive feedback and maybe write to them in person. Remember, the candidate you turned down could well be your future client! Just think, how would you want your daughter dealt with if she was unsuccessful!

- **Holding hands during resignation and after start date.** This is arguably THE most dangerous time in the recruitment process! Yes, it's true! You've interviewed your candidate and they have accepted your offer, but the start date is two or four weeks ahead! Your agency should keep in touch on your behalf during this period, making sure that your new employee is still fully 'engaged'. Remember other (unscrupulous) recruiters will not take heed of your candidates situation! They will still keep offering them opportunities before AND after start date. Your agency should retain some gentle contact on your behalf and provide feedback in the early days of the employee's tenure. Check that they know how to do this effectively.

- **Post commencement support.** Building on the above point; I suggest that the agency provides you with a 'report' during the first three months of the new employment. Ideally they should work with you and/or your HR team to ensure that challenges are dealt with early and that any mismatches are recognised early on. A monthly visit on site is an ideal opportunity to discuss such matters.

- **Process Review.** Complacency is a true killer, in any relationship. Recruitment is no different. I urge that you invite your agency to meet with you after your candidate has commenced with you to discuss the process from 'both sides' and to establish how things can improve next time! Nothing is perfect, so use this to learn how YOU can improve your systems too. Did you interview properly, was feedback relevant, is the induction course as described? Be prepared to learn some 'home truths' but recognise that this feedback is crucial in developing your own ability to hire effectively.

- **Temporary and contract staff.** This is NOT a book about the pros and cons and merits of temporary staff and contract personnel. I would however suggest that you establish if your chosen agency can support you with such staff. They are very useful as they can often 'plug the hole' quickly on a short or long term basis. The process tends to be faster, and you can often negotiate the rate you pay, but remember the agency is paying employers' National Insurance Contributions on your behalf, running the payroll AND providing you with credit. Knock them down too low and the quality WILL suffer. If the agency suggests that the temp is SELF EMPLOYED, be very careful! The rule of thumb is currently that unless the temp has multiple sources of income (at any ONE time), has a genuine reason NOT to be self employed, then they should be PAYE. IT contactors and some engineers operate outside this framework. I suggest you discuss this with your accountant or professional advisor.

The above are the main features offered by mainstream recruiters today. There are however, other services provided by more specialist recruiters:-

- Personality or psychometric testing

- Interim managers

- Out sourced HR services

- Master vendor agreements

- Facilities management

So, which type of recruitment organisation is right for you?

With over 18,000 recruitment businesses in the UK, there are 3 main categories:-

Search and Selection

For those who wish to hire a marketing manager with experience of say, the Chinese Telecoms market, popping an advert in the local press will be a complete waste of time. Recruitment organisations that recruit for such positions are in the Search and Selection sector. The search organisation will usually either develop a short list based upon knowledge of the sector, an established database and current research via a network of contacts. This type of recruitment campaign rarely uses advertising as a method of establishing a short list-although more and more search organisations are blending this methodology with their historic approach.

The selection recruitment business may use a day-to-day database to identify 'your candidate' but will also invariably place an advert on the Internet, in the specialised trade journal or one of the broadsheet newspapers, such as The Times or The Guardian. They will take your brief, and develop an advert with your approval, which will often display your brand image or logo (occasionally a client may wish to advertise anonymously for confidential reasons such as they do not want the competition to know what they are up to or perhaps they are replacing somebody who does not know they are about to get the bullet!) The selection agency will place the advertisement on your behalf and deal with the response using your company name or their own.

Head Hunters

Head hunters operate in a twilight world! Or so the rumour goes. Actually, true head hunters usually only work at senior or board level of major organisations. They are invariably engaged by the employer to approach a limited number of high calibre individuals. The employer normally already has the short list in mind and the head-hunter is required to be discreet and consultative. Head hunters are usually very well connected and might come from an industry specific background. They often require a retainer in advance of any work commenced.

Specialist (corporate and independent)

Whether you are looking for a finance manager, a logistics specialist or an account manager within the petro-chemicals sector; the specialist recruitment sector is a viable alternative to search and selection organisations (however, just to make things *really* confusing, many search and selection firms *are* specialists themselves; it is just that they operate on a different basis to the organisations discussed here). These recruitment businesses mostly charge upon results (known as contingency) although (here we go again) some *do* charge on a stage payment basis! Confusing, isn't it?

A good example of the specialist sector is accountancy. In the UK there are a large number of specialists that recruit specifically for this sector. In addition to the large multi branch organisations that may be able to offer a nationwide, European or even Global service, there are many excellent independent recruitment organisations with only one or a few offices. Such businesses often offer the opportunity to work closely with one of the directors of the recruitment organisation (or at least a highly motivated manager). Such people usually have industry specific experience and/or contacts built up over the years. Unlike the multi-branch organisations, such recruiters usually have lower overheads and *may* pass on such savings to their clients.

Other fields that are serviced by specialist recruitment organisations include:- legal, medical, finance, banking, insurance, sales, oil and gas, retail, construction, catering, etc.

High Street (corporate and independent)

Interestingly (and confusingly), many so called high street recruitment organisations are well equipped to cover some areas of specialisation also *but* they are also able to provide more generic office, industrial, driving and catering staff. Most such businesses offer a service based purely upon results and provide staff on both a permanent and temporary basis. In the UK there are many well-known 'high street' names such as Reed, Blue Arrow and Manpower who offer a nationwide service (many also have specialist divisions such as Reed Accountancy). Additionally, in most towns and all cities across the UK, Australia, South Africa, Europe and North America there are a large number of independents (many with just one or two offices) that offer local contacts, personal service and value for money. Whilst such an agency will not be able to offer a global service or necessarily have access to a database of Dutch speaking paralegals or off shore tax specialists, they will have access to local talent, contacts within the local business community and will have an detailed knowledge of local salaries. Additionally, staff in such recruitment organisations are often exceptionally motivated and you may well end up dealing with one of the owners of the business.

How to choose *your* recruitment organisation?

Before we get on to the all-important point of fees and guarantees, it is important to weigh other aspects. Assuming that you have decided which *type* of recruitment organisation fits your requirements; who do you choose? Gut feel has its place of course, but consider the following:-

- **Who will work on my campaign?** Will it be the person who came to meet you (the manager perhaps or senior consultant) or will it be someone else? Ensure that if your campaign is *not* to be handled be the person you initially met, is the person that deals with your needs capable of handling your needs effectively. Too often the business is 'won' by a senior member of staff only to be 'palmed off' onto some else more junior or less experienced. Sure, rookies need to learn but will they be coached by a more experienced person? In certain situations, your initial contact will hand over the relationship to a *more* experienced person or possibly a specialist. It is **vital** however, to ensure that whoever does actually work on your campaign has sufficient information and really does understand your needs. This may demand a second meeting with other consultants *after* you have awarded your business to your chosen recruitment organisation. Or maybe, you *defer* the decision until you have met all the members of the team who will work on your account.

- **Does the recruitment organisation have the relevant experience?** This may well sound silly but are you happy to rely upon an organisation to provide you with all important 100 warehouse staff in the run up towards Christmas when their largest account has, up until now, only demanded 10 temporaries? I am not saying *don't* award such a contract to a relatively small supplier, (indeed they may work *incredibly* hard to prove your faith in them, seeing the opportunity as a gateway to larger accounts!) simply ensure that you have done sufficient due diligence to satisfy yourself that they are prepared, willing and able to support your organisation.

- **Do they actually understand your needs?** This point cannot be stressed enough. Does the consultant that will recruit for you actually understand not only what the role is about but also what experience you are looking for? Get them to explain to you in *their* own words, exactly what *they* believe they should be looking for. Does their understanding match yours? If not, educate and inform them. Most experienced recruitment consultants are used to asking detailed questions to build up a thorough picture of what their clients are looking for. Some clients, having made the decision as to who will carry out their campaign, will request that the recruitment firm submits a detailed proposal regarding their understanding of needs (more of this later).

- **What level of priority will they give this campaign?** This is often overlooked. The client awards the business to a recruitment organisation that seems delighted with the decision, but then hears little from the agency! Find out how many other campaigns or clients the recruitment company is likely to be handling at the same time as yours. Are you a priority or just another number? If you have *specific* needs, are you one of several organisations that will be competing for the agencies 'best' candidates? Is 'your' consultant overworked? How quickly does the recruitment firm think it can start working on your campaign and how fast does it believe that it can produce results? Discover which other organisations the recruitment agency is working with. Will you get the 'pick of the crop' or the just 'windfalls'?

- **Confidentiality and the competition.** Whilst discussing your organisation, the role you are offering, the culture and future prospects; you will probably find yourself telling the recruitment consultant in front of you a great deal about your business ("sharing", I think our American cousins call it!). Before you disclose any sensitive information, find out if the recruitment firm you are entertaining recruits for any of your competitors (nothing wrong with that and *can* be proof of expertise and good standing) and ensure that where appropriate you advise them of any areas of confidentiality that should be recognised. In my experience, most recruitment consultants are discreet and can keep a commercial secret. If you are very nervous, get the recruitment firm to sign a confidentiality agreement. It won't help much if they spill the beans but at least it will let them know that you are serious.

- **Do they 'get us'?** This is important. In addition to the details about the role and your 'ideal' candidate profile; does the recruitment consultant *actually understand* what type of company you are? Sure, things *do* get lost in translation, but more people aren't recruited because they 'don't fit in' rather than have mismatched skills. Don't get me wrong here; I'm **not** talking about discrimination! I'm referring to a candidate's understanding of the company's approach to customer service, quality or excellence (not to mention 'hard work'). Ensure that the recruitment organisation you engage 'gets you'!

- **Are they members of any professional organisation and are their staff qualified?** Qualifications and training alone do not a great organisation make; but I'm *not* aware of many support service firms or those in the professions such as the legal or accountancy sectors who *do not* train their staff to recognised standards or who do not belong to the appropriate professional body. In the UK, the REC (Recruitment & Employment Confederation) provides both corporate and individual membership status to organisations and individuals that are genuinely committed to providing exceptional service. Additionally the REC offers a large number of training courses and examinations leading to industry recognised qualifications. Is the recruitment organisation a quality assured company with accreditation such as ISO EN 9000 or does it have its own quality standards that it strives to adhere to? Are they an Investor in People accredited company? If not, how do they train, develop and assess their own staff? Avoiding the villains is simple if you ask the right questions.

- **Can I get any testimonial references to back up their claims?** Most recruitment firms will be happy to supply written testimonials confirming their past successes. These are useful, but dig further. Ask if you can have the telephone numbers of the referees plus some additional contacts within organisations that the recruitment organisation is recruiting for *right now*. Past success does not imply future excellence. Just make sure that you are dealing with a firm that is *still* up to scratch and not one that is trading upon yesterday's success stories!

How much to pay?

As the owner of a recruitment business for twenty five years I have had to justify my organisation's fees on many occasions. Interestingly I have also used other providers of recruitment services myself when I have been unable to identify suitable candidates via my own company's efforts or for more specialised staff. Additionally, before I started my own recruitment business I had used the services of 'high street' recruitment agencies. I am, therefore, suitably qualified to comment on agency fees and what is appropriate.

So, what to pay? As with most things in commercial life, there are no hard and fast rules, there are however some guide lines that should be observed. From the outsider's point of view, recruitment agency fees can be perceived to be quite expensive; between 10% & 30% depending on the area of specialisation and service provided. This may initially seem like a great deal of money; however if we are used to paying accountants and lawyers between £100 and £300 per hour for a professional service, why not then to a recruitment organisation? After all, is the task of sourcing a crucial member of the company not as vital as obtaining legal or taxation advice?

The trouble is that unlike lawyers, accountants and IT consultants; most recruitment businesses do not charge by the hour, but upon results only. Not unlike those people everybody 'loves to hate'- estate agents! If recruitment organisations were able to charge by the hour, their fees would be dramatically less. At present, however, the fees you pay to a recruitment organisation also covers work conducted on behalf of other organisations that do not result in a fee being charged.

You could argue that you only want to pay for the work they do on your behalf, but until the work industry reinvents itself and charges by the hour, this will not be possible.

Search and Selection and Head Hunters' Fees

The above not with standing, *specialist* recruitment organisations such as search & selection agencies and head hunters will often break their fees down in to three stage payments, the first two to cover administrative work, research and short-listing procedures, the third payable upon results. These payments may or may not have guarantees or conditions attached. Additionally advertising is often charged by such agencies to their clients, irrespective of results.

Search and selection organisations usually charge $1/3^{rd}$ for commencing work on an assignment, $1/3^{rd}$ for providing a short list and $1/3^{rd}$ upon successful appointment. The two initial charges will rarely have any rebates or guarantees attached. You are paying for the consultant's time. The third and final payment will usually have a guarantee attached and possible a financial rebate.

These firms will charge anything between 20% and 30% of the new employee's salary-including a provision for car, pension, commission or bonuses.

If the recruitment firm places an advert via a media-buying agency, it will often negotiate a discount. This may be passed on to you, or they may charge you the full price and a handling charge. A discount, if offered, will rarely be more than 10%. Such charges may be due upon the advertisement appearing or deferred until the commencement of a new employee.

Specialist recruitment organisations' fees

These firms will charge anything between 10% and 30% depending upon supply and demand, additional services offered and guarantees but may blend their fee structure with that of the Search & Selection sector.

Generalist recruitment organisations' fees

Most generalist and 'high street agencies' will tend to charge between 10% and 25% depending upon any areas of expertise they confess to have, the areas of specialisation, added value services and the financial rebate or replacement guarantees offered. For the most part they will charge the client upon what's known as a contingency basis; that is, payment on results.

Guarantees and Payment Terms

Whilst it is important to negotiate a 'fair fee', it is, I believe, probably more important to ensure that you negotiate a guarantee that gives you **REAL** security in case things 'go wrong'. In my own recruitment business, we provide our clients with a sliding scale of fees that ensure our clients can protect their investment with a free replacement guarantee of up to 2 years. This is exceptional, and whilst indicative of the confidence we have in our candidates it also means that our clients have confidence in us. If things go 'wrong' for any reason, at Orchard we 'do it again'...for nothing! I strongly recommend that you focus more on getting an extended free replacement guarantee than on the fee itself. Value for money is not just about the fee but what happens if it goes 'wrong'. Most agencies will offer an element of rebate instead of a free replacement. Look hard at what's on offer. Is the money back guarantee acceptable? Can you get a better deal? If the agency is confident in their processes then get them to put their money where their mouth is. I suggest that 100% in the first week, 75% in week two, 50% in week three and 25% in week four are very average and that you can negotiate better!

Additionally, consider payment terms. Is the agency offering 28 days terms or better? Is the payment term from **START** date or date of invoice? Make sure you know and comply with the payment terms because if you ARE LATE, you will find the agency's guarantees are invalid! It is YOUR prerogative to comply. Don't lose out just because your accounts team have failed to send the payment off on time. Seriously, watch this like a hawk. It can save you heartache!

Temporary staff fees and temp to perm deals

'Try before you buy' is a great way of ensuring that what you want is 'fit for purpose' before you make a commitment. Staff are no different! Would you buy a car without a test drive? Of course not! If a candidate is not working then why not offer them the opportunity to 'temp' before a formal offer is made. This way you get the chance to see how they perform and they get the chance to establish whether they feel comfortable. Of course, a week or two is not going to give both parties sufficient information to make a bullet proof appraisal of mutual suitability; but it's a great start.

If you can put the staff on your own payroll or via an agency, you should still expect to pay the agency introduction fee. The fee, however, may be open to re-negotiation subject to the gross profit the agency derives from the assignment. It is not unreasonable to expect a discount from the standard permanent introduction fee if you have had a temporary worker via the agency. Just make sure you are not paying twice!

So, what's a reasonable fee?

It is important to say that no specific percentage or amount of money is 'the right fee'. Remember certain appointments are highly specialised and at any given time, there may be only a dozen or so people in the whole country that could fill this position. It would be impossible for the owner or manager of a business to gain experience needed to research the market – the time to develop the up to date contacts to know 'who is hot and who is not'. In this instance you have little choice- after you have exhausted the options discussed previously you have little option then to engage the services of such a recruitment organisation. But for how much?

Search and selection agencies used to be 'old school' and were not prepared to negotiate at all. Today they are more flexible. Being a tough negotiator is one thing-but you can drive the price down so much that the consultant then has little incentive to work on your assignment. Remember you may pay a fee of 25% of £60k, i.e. £15k, but 'your' consultant is unlikely to see much of that, he has to contribute towards expenses, office costs, computer equipment, support staff, directors salaries etc etc. Having said this, whilst such fees are not cheap, recruiting the right person can dramatically impact a company's performance. If you still believe that the fee is too high or there is no room for negotiation, then find out what added value services the recruitment agency can provide, such as personality profiling or maybe a money back guarantee if the new recruit does not work out as expected. As previously discussed, don't simply accept the initial rebate offered; try to negotiate a reducing amount over 3,6 or even 12 months. Remember if recruitment agencies do their job properly there should be no reason why they shouldn't put their money where their mouth is, especially when it comes to high fee/high salary biased placements.

Selection agency fees are subject to the same rules of some with one exception. They will usually charge you for the advertisement placed on your behalf, so do make sure you are happy with it and try to have some input in to the advert. Would you respond to it yourself? Ask your colleagues or the perhaps the person currently doing the job. Ask the agency why they have selected that magazine, website, media or paper. Get them to justify themselves- have they used them before and to what success. Again consider guarantees and rebates.

Negotiating with non search and selection agencies

In general, most non-search and selection agencies charge between 10% and 25%. Supposing you are looking for a secretary earning £18,000. The fees could range from £1,800 to £4,500. How to get better value? In any negotiation we are taught to try to obtain a 'win win'. However the line between 'win win' and 'win lose' is a fine one and it is important to remember that even if the agency did come up with your perfect candidate within 24 hours they still have done what you have asked of them. Which would you rather; your dentist remove your pain in one quick half an hour session or would you feel you had gained better value for money if he took two hours of drilling & filling!

Do not begrudge an agency their fee if they work quickly and efficiently. I have lost count of the number of times that clients have disputed a fee when we have pulled out all the stops to find their perfect candidate; spending hours trawling databases in search of specific skills, taking references, assessing skills and seeing people outside of office hours. Interestingly, clients rarely complain about fees if their campaign has been protracted; several months passing before the perfect candidate is found but the client feels he has had value for money. How strange!

The most important thing to consider is that by driving down the fees too aggressively with, perhaps a non-senior recruitment consultant, you may be the one who loses out in the end! Imagine *you* had two clients looking for the same product, but with one paying a higher fee. Who would *you* look after better? Who would you give first choice to? If you really believe that staff are a commodity, then this does not apply to you! But, if you recognise that not all candidates are 'equal' and the recruitment agency gets to decide who they send their better candidates to, then make sure that your recruitment agency is sufficiently incentivised to give *you* the choice you deserve!

Cost Comparisons

Let's face it; there is an element of 'sales' in the recruitment process; convincing the employer to use an agency as opposed to the 'DIY' method.

This is NOT the place to 'sell' you the idea of using an agency, however it is worth pointing out the list of 'steps' that you 'should' take to recruit effectively yourself. 'Clever' sales people use this as a 'cost vs. time comparison'. I consider that if you are reading then you are both intelligent and well informed and you would see through such a 'smoke screen' immediately. So, let's just consider exactly what you need to do to go it completely 'alone'. The costs associated to such activities can only be allocated by you...

- Develop job description and person specification

- Choose media for advertising

- Place ads on www or specialist/local press

- Mount Social Media campaign

- Deal with all incoming applications

- Respond immediately to interested parties

- Create short list

- Invite short listed candidates for interview

- Arrange IT/Skills tests

- Plan interviews

- Conduct initial interviews

- Provide feedback and disengage with unsuccessful candidates

- Arrange second interviews

- Make offer and send letters and contracts

- Arrange induction course

Chapter Five

Getting the Best From Your Recruitment Agency

It has been my observation that few organisations understand exactly how to get the best from the recruitment agency they are working with. Having decided to engage a recruitment agency, many employers fail to communicate what they are REALLY looking for, avoid creating a satisfactory person specification or job description and then refuse to call their agency back when they call to present a candidate! Why?

By using an agency an employer can save a significant amount of time (and therefore money) and ultimately the organisation can usually recruit a better quality candidate via an agency than if they use the DIY approach. The pool of candidates that the agency has access to will, inevitably, be much larger than any employer has access to. Additionally the agency is incentivised to work hard at sourcing the very best candidates for their client. Of course, as of writing, there is a glut in the number of candidates available-and yet, the quality and suitability of candidates is often very disappointing. Employers today want exceptional candidates that add real value to their organisation. This will upset some readers, and of course it is a generalisation; but many of the candidates who apply to recruitment adverts have been 'culled' in redundancy programs that have identified them as employees that are not really 'up to scratch'! And which employer wants someone else's cast offs? No, the best people, in any market are often working, and in difficult times, these high calibre candidates are usually 'staying put' and not actively looking! They need identifying and proactively recruiting by a third party who can 'sell' your opportunity to them. A recruitment organisation will no doubt have an extensive database, but will also spend time and resources developing an understanding of candidates who are 'off the radar'. And because these candidates are not actively looking, the employer will not usually have to out bid each other or compete with other parties; except the candidate's existing employer of course!

The situation becomes even worse when it comes to school/college leavers and dare I say it, even graduates. The number of under 25s that I have encountered over the last decade who lack basic literacy & IT skills beggars belief! This is not about to turn into a rant about the standard of education in the UK; I will only say that finding articulate, literate youngsters is incredibly hard work. Any employer recruiting a trainee on their own behalf will find it galling.

A reputable recruitment agency should be able to evidence a track record of success. Ask what their interview to offer ratio is, how much experience they have in 'your sector', what they do to source candidates and also what guarantees they provide? Specifically, do they offer free replacement guarantees or money back rebates? Of course, I'm biased but what I am about to say is true! Do not work too hard at negotiating your agency fee down 'too much'. You may congratulate yourself in your negotiating skills but end up missing out.

Giving your vacancy to too many agencies will often backfire on you! If the agency is paid upon results rather than on a retained basis, the agencies will rarely spend much time on your campaign. They'd rather work on a position whereupon they will know that they'll get paid if they find you a suitable candidate rather than accepting say a 1in 3 or 1 in 5 chance of getting paid. As far as my own agency is concerned, we rarely accept assignments competing with more than one other agency. It's not that we don't relish competition, it's simply that we only have a limited number of hours a day and therefore we'd rather focus on clients who are loyal to us and who we know that we're likely to be able to recruit for. Why work on a role that you only have a 20% or 25% chance of filling compared to one where you have a 100% or 50% chance of earning a fee? Loyal clients are also most likely to be offered first pick of exceptional candidates. It makes sense...

These are my 'Top Tips' for success to getting the best out of a recruitment agency.

- Provide a detailed job description and person specification
- Return the calls to the agency; they will only be in contact to obtain

more information or to advise you of an exceptional candidate

- Arrange to interview candidates promptly otherwise you may miss out

- Don't negotiate too aggressively; you might not end up being 'top of the list'

- Ask the agency to evidence their 'success ratio' and experience within your 'sector'

- Do not give your vacancy to too many agencies; you won't be taken seriously and might end up at the bottom of everyone's list.

Chapter Six

Advertising

Whilst this chapter is not meant to be the final word in creative writing or a guide to the legalities of advert writing, I do aim to give you some solid advice that will not only produce decent results but will also keep you out of trouble! I have also included some essential tips on how to go about dealing with advertising response and arranging the initial interview.

Where to Advertise

The media that you choose for a specific advertisement will of course depend very much upon the role that you are trying to fill. Other criteria will include the location of the business, the budget and matters of confidentiality.

Let's assume for the moment that your business is located in a busy city or town and that you are looking to recruit for office support staff. Such roles could include reception, secretarial, sales order processing, accounts clerks etc. There is a very good chance that your business will have a natural catchment area from within which you should be able to recruit such staff. This area will probably be served by at least one, if not several, local newspapers. The best way to establish which is the most effective paper for you is by obtaining several weeks worth of each publication and trawling through the recruitment pages to establish which paper has the most recruitment advertising and more specifically, if appropriate, which newspaper covers the vacancies that you are trying to fill. For example, one local newspaper may be more inclined to carry middle management vacancies compared to another which may be for less senior positions.

Having drawn your own conclusions as to which is the dominant or most appropriate newspaper for you, you need more information. Firstly, establish what the circulation for each newspaper is. This may be somewhat confusing because, whilst most local newspapers are obliged to report their circulation figures, the freely distributed press will naturally report greater circulation numbers than its paid for local competitor. It can be argued that whilst a 'freebie' could well have three times the circulation, it actually has less readership than a paid for publication because those that pay their own money to own a paid for publication are more committed to reading it than those who simply receive a copy through the door gratis every week, which either ends up in the shredder or at the bottom of the cat litter tray!

So how do you find out which is the most effective paper for you when confronted by various alternatives? Trial and error of course is the most effective methodology, but, for most organisations is an expensive method of research. Probably the best way to obtain such vital intelligence is to pick up the phone and speak to the people who have placed adverts in these various newspapers for roles that are not dissimilar to yours. As long as you are up front about your reason for calling, most managers are prepared to share such information (as long as you are not a direct competitor of theirs, of course).

Whilst talking with these managers also enquire how much it actually cost them to place the advert. I will come on to this later in more detail, however, the so called rate card charge that is published by newspapers in their 'media packs' is not necessarily the price that you may expect to pay. It will become apparent when doing research that some organisations obtain a preferential rate compared to others who pay the full amount!

Another great way of working out which publication to choose is to ask those in your current organisation which local papers they read themselves. This information is crucial, particularly if you live outside the catchment area yourself. Talking of catchment areas, what exactly do we mean by this? It is dangerous to come up with a definitive radius within which people will be assumed to be looking for local work and ignoring those outside. However, it is a fair assumption that the higher the salary or the more specialised the role, the further afield people will travel for work. In my humble experience those working at positions of lower than, say, junior management prefer to work within 30 minutes travel time of their home location, except of course, when they have the opportunity of working in a large town or city, whereupon they may consider up to 90 minutes travelling, to be offset by the cachet of working in such an environment or the financial rewards.

An additional method of establishing which is the appropriate local newspaper for your campaign is by asking your counterparts in the local chamber of commerce, trading association, or business club. Your organisation may operate out of premises where there are various other employers such as business parks, industrial estates and serviced offices. When passing pleasantries in the car park, why not discuss this subject? It will be time well invested.

Specialist and Management Positions

Many of the above rules also apply to more specialist or senior positions. In whichever area of commercial activity your business is involved (or indeed the public sector) there will be one or more trade publications that cover it. You will be amazed by the titles of some of these diverse publications, many of them so amusingly featured in the BBC TV programme Have I Got News For You. If you are seeking a specialist with experience within, say, the manufacture of aluminium extrusions, salmon fishery production or the import of frozen foods from Europe, there is likely to be at least one publication that you can advertise within. Such publications are also likely to hold adverts from specialist recruitment organisations who (may) be experts in your sector. I know for example of several recruitment organisations that only recruit within the packaging sector. They are often staffed by those who have previously worked in such a field and *should* have current contacts within their field of specialisation. Game keepers turned poachers if you will!

Whether you use specialist press or specialist recruitment organisations for your recruitment campaigns, it is important to realise that they are just that; specialists. Do not use them for more generic roles. There is no point placing an advert in a specialist press which has a readership of perhaps only several thousand every month across the whole country when you are looking for a generic office administrator who lives within a mile of your premises!

Similarly, there are a variety of specialist publications that relate to specific roles as opposed to industries. For example the accountancy profession, sales and marketing, engineering and legal are all well served by their own professional or institute magazines and newspapers. Whilst an advert in the local press may suffice for a generic credit controller, a finance director may well only be looking in the specific professional publications covering their sector.

The Internet

Many of the rules regarding which newspaper or publication to advertise in also apply to the Internet. There are a vast number of Internet websites alleging that they are *the* place to attract staff. The problem is, in my experience, that many of these web boards are anything but effective and may cost you a fortune (and time) to trial. Most local newspapers have a link to their own (or associated) website as do many specialist trade publications. For some of the latter, you may pay an additional fee over and above that of placing an initial printed advert.

Wherever possible, endeavour to obtain evidence that the website in question is successful; especially when dealing with high cost, trade specific, websites.

For more generic recruitment, as above, ask around. Where would friends and family look for a job? The fact is that the Internet has become an incredibly powerful way of finding a new position and therefore equally powerful to those wishing to employ staff.

If you consider the UK mainland, for example, there are an increasingly huge number of websites to choose from. In my experience different regions seem to be served better by specific websites than other websites at different times of the year, depending upon the marketing that the website in question is engaged in. In particular its search engine optimisation strategy! My own organisation has used a large number of sites such as Office Recruit, Reed, Go Job Site, Total Jobs, Monster etc, etc. We have experienced differing results for identical vacancies for clients based in different locations. Again, there have been differing results depending upon the time of year. It is difficult to be precise therefore, but some general research and discussions with those operating the websites can bear fruit. Which leads me on to the next point, how much to pay?

What to Pay

The first rule to remember is that almost everything, when it comes to advertising, is subject to negotiation. Whilst there are several publications, that because of their monopolistic or pre-eminent position in either their geographical location or standing in their specific trade or profession, are in the enviable position of having little or no competition and are likely to meet your attempts at obtaining a discount with a firm refusal; almost all other publications or websites are prepared to discuss some form of negotiation.

Local newspapers are often vying for advertising revenue, especially if they are one of several in their market place. Whilst they will invariably quote you a 'rate card' price based upon an amount per column centimetre (ie the price of each centimetre in depth per column width of *that* specific publication), there are often deals to be done. Remember when comparing quotations that different publications may have different column widths and £10 per column centimetre in one publication may well be more expensive then £13 per column centimetre in another publication. Also, if having carried out the research detailed above, you still have little to choose between which publications to advertise in, consider the circulation figures. If one publication has twice the circulation of the other, it may well be better value for money if its column centimetre price is less than double that of its competitor.

If there is little to choose between publications and pricing comparisons, why not play one off against the other and see if you can get a more favourable rate? Different publications will have different deadline dates and times. It is therefore useful to understand this information as a deal can often be struck with a newspaper looking to fill its pages just before the deadline. If your publication of choice often prints duplicate adverts, it is because they are struggling to find sufficient genuine paying adverts.

Another strategy in addition to a reduced price per column centimetre is to request a larger advert for the same price, a reduced price for the second or third week (or month) that it appears or a better position. It is widely accepted (in the West) that the top right hand corner of any publication is the preferred position in which to appear. It is not unreasonable to request this position. Similarly some publications offer spot colour, whereby red, for example, may be used for some or all of your advert. This is normally charged as extra, but you may be able to get this thrown in for nothing or at a reduced price. Paying for such press advertising should be simple. Many publications will accept a credit card (and then send you a VAT invoice) whilst others may offer to open an account for you. Remember that opening an account may take some time and if you wish your advert to appear immediately, you may need to wait until this process has been completed.

Internet websites are a little different in that (for the most part) they are able to publish (or post, to use the correct terminology) details of your vacancy immediately. Unless you are intending to advertise multiple vacancies, the websites are not as enthusiastic at discounting their rates. The reason is that this new media is gaining in effectiveness and is winning the war against traditional media such as local or specialist press. It is, of course, worth discussing a discount, however don't expect too much. The more effective the website, the less of a discount you are likely to be offered.

When running multiple campaigns, it is always a good idea to try different sites and monitor their effectiveness. Don't put all your eggs in one basket until you're certain which is the best one for your specific needs.

Many website job boards will permit you to update your advert on a daily basis. By changing several words, your advert will often get moved to the 'top of the page' again. The higher up you are, the more effective your campaign will be.

The Advertisement Itself

There have been some fantastic books written on advertising (Ogilvy on Advertising & Words That Sell by Ted Nicholas, for example) that I would strongly urge you to sample, but the best advice I can give you about writing great recruitment advertisement copy is to spend a couple of hours carrying out your own research. Grab a selection of local newspapers and the recruitment sections of the Broadsheet press, pour yourself a coffee and prepare to be amazed! Most advertisements are so poorly written that it's any wonder that they receive any response at all. They are unimaginative, uninformative and uninspiring!

Look at the adverts with the eyes of an applicant, *not* as an employer. Job hunters are interested in 'What's in it for them'. Any advert has to act like the trailer to a film; it must grab the audience's attention, inform, educate and make a call to action! Most adverts are dull, drab and leave the reader wondering what's really on offer. The fact is that advertising, whether in newsprint or the Internet, is expensive; outrageously so if the results are less than required. If you are spending money on advertising, for goodness sake, make it work for you!

Most adverts are thrown together by people with little or no experience in creative writing....and it shows! Imagine the scene, Debbie the receptionist hands in her notice to the Managing Director on Monday morning (why is it ALWAYS Monday morning?). The MD calls his secretary and "Debbie's leaving, get an advert in the paper". Now whilst the secretary can write a decent letter and is grammatically competent, she may not necessarily be the best person to *write* the advert.

As with the development of the job specification, get some of the people who are involved in the role to have some input into the development of the advert and take your time. It's better to miss an advert deadline rather than waste your time and money by placing an advert that is ineffective, only to be followed up by a better advert the next week that is ignored by the 'perfect candidate' who was put off by the original, poorly drafted version. Measure twice, cut once and get the result you want.

Think about the advert from the candidates' point of view. Will it appeal? Will it inform? As of writing the UK, USA and Europe are experiencing 'challenging economics times' with increasing high levels of unemployment. Despite the glut of candidates available, many organisations are unhappy with the calibre of applications. Every organisation wants to recruit 'exceptional' staff. The chance is that your advert, whether for a specialist or more generalist role, will be competing for the interest of *your* new employee.

This is how many adverts are written:-

Secretary
New Town
An opportunity has arisen for a secretary to join widget export team. You'll support the Director of this busy department. You must be well organised, articulate and used to producing work of a high standard. Excellent references required. Salary subject to experience.

Apply Mr Jones, Director
ABC Company
123 The Street etc

Well of course "an opportunity has arisen", why on earth would the company be advertising if it had no need? Remember, words cost money. Choose them wisely. The above and its equivalents appear in their masses every week, and generate poor response. There is nothing *essentially* wrong with the advert of course, and in-fact in times of high unemployment, this advert could produce reasonable results, but in today's employment market, any advert must *really* stand out.

Of course, any advert must comply with all relevant legislation regarding discrimination based upon sex, race, religion, sexual orientation and in many countries in the world, age. There are, of course, certain exceptions to rule, such as the right, for example, of a women's refuge to employ only women. Details of such exemptions may be sought from the Commission of Racial Equality in the UK.

Any advert should comprise the following components:-

- **Job Title**

- **Location**

- **Salary and Benefits**

- **Brief company profile**

- **Overview of duties and responsibilities**

- **Person specification and requirements**

- **Call to action**

- **Contact details**

This is a much better advert, looked at from the job hunters' point of view

Export Director's Secretary
Central New Town
£18, 000 to £20,000
5 weeks holiday plus bonus

We are a seven year old company manufacturing specialist electronic components for the automotive sector with smart, modern, air conditioned premises and a staff of 45.Working closely with our dynamic Export Director, your duties will include client contact (by phone and face to face), travel arrangements, diary management, preparing sales proposals and producing detailed sales analysis. We require a confident, experienced secretary with intermediate IT skills including Excel, Word and PowerPoint with an accurate typing speed of 60wpm

Apply to John Browne at Electro Bits UK
020 7333 1111
j.browne@electrobits.co.uk
www.electrobits.co.uk
www.facebook.com/electrobits

So, why is this advert better?

- Specific Director's secretary. The Finance Director will invariably be a different character to the Export Director and whilst the job content *may be broadly similar,* the style of communication and specific work will be very different

- Central New Town. Be specific regarding the location

- Provide the salary range; it stimulates interest

- Identify specific benefits; in this case 5 weeks holiday PLUS bonus

- Establish stability of company by explaining how long established. Job seekers especially administrators and technical people, look for such reassurances

- Explain the type of offices. Air conditioning is increasingly sought after as a non-taxable benefit (give the government time, however!)

- Expand upon the generic job title, in this case explaining that client contact is crucial. Shrinking violets need NOT apply!

- Be specific re skills and speeds

- Provide various methods of contact. Make it easy to apply

This advert provides sufficient information about the company and the role for a candidate to make a decision as to whether they should apply or not. It also offers a 'call to action'. It is *not* too wordy or filled with jargon. It is designed to get people to apply, but only if they are suitable. Which is the better advert? The one that produces 100 responses (but only 5 from suitable applicant) or the one that produces 10 responses (but only 3 from suitable applicants)? I would strongly argue **the latter** as it is more efficient and has not generated interest from time wasters or unsuitable applicants who need responding to! Some may disagree with me, and I appreciate their views but I wonder how many times *they* have had to write 'rejection' letters and emails. Of course, you could decide *not* to respond to the unsuitable applicants; but I would suggest that such a decision is inappropriate. Not only is it discourteous, but it does not help with the development of your company's profile in the local/ business community. Ignore the warehouseman that applies who is unsuitable and his daughter is unlikely to apply for the sales position you offer a year later!

As of writing this book, there is talk as to whether it is appropriate to request a hand written covering letter or not (as it may discriminate against those who have poor handwriting or dyslexia), whether it is appropriate to state that a specific grade of qualification is essential or not (does it necessarily follow that a person who did not gain GCSE grade C at English, will **not** be able to spell properly? Maybe they are affected by bad nerves during exams!). I believe that a CV *should* be *expected*, but I have personally met many people over the years, who for whatever reason, have not had a CV, and have been totally suitable for the position they applied for. I can think of one individual who applied for a position as a Class I driver, who had been made redundant after 10 years' service. He walked through our door, we took references over the telephone (which were exceptional) and called our client immediately. He was interviewed that afternoon and started the next day! Days spent out of employment? One! Would the driver had been more employable if he had had a CV with him? No. Would the client have been better prepared if he had seen the candidate's CV in advance? Possibly. The most important thing was that the client knew what he was looking for and was prepared to arrange an interview as a result of our recommendation. (for those of you snorting about un-professionalism, the client in question is a very large logistics company who got the candidate to complete their own application form upon the candidates arrival and they took up their own references, the offer of employment being made subject to them of course).

Chapter Seven

Response Handling, Short Listing and Other Important Pre-Interview Activities

Response Handling

Handling the response from candidates is a crucial part of the recruitment process; unfortunately it is one that many employers (and recruiters) get dreadfully wrong. The good news is that with some basic planning the process can be simplified. If using a website to generate candidate interest via email, then allocate ONE individual to the task of acknowledging that you have received their application, and what the next step is. And actually DO have a series of 'next steps'...!

If the applicant is clearly unsuitable, then advise them by return. I would suggest that you avoid a dialogue with unsuccessful applicants; it serves little purpose and avoids any unpleasantness. Remember that any communication with candidates is an opportunity to communicate with a wider public. Fast effective communication, even if advising that their application has not been successful, is likely to engender a positive feeling about your organisation. Slow, inefficient or even zero communication (especially when an application is unsuccessful) will create the opposite effect. And remember, a disgruntled applicant WILL tell lots of people about their experience with your company. And who are these people? I'll tell you! People with friends, partners, parents, and children...people who might be YOUR existing clients or suppliers! Be very careful how you communicate. Remember the power of social media sites and good old-fashioned 'word of mouth'. It can build your reputation, but it can destroy your reputation too.

If the applicant is suitable then advise that you are placing them on the 'short list' or arrange for them to come in for interview. Do not prevaricate;

even in challenging economic times, talent is in great demand! If applicants apply in writing (from an off line advert for example) then call them to arrange an interview; don't just write back. It takes way too long.

Short Listing

Whether using a recruitment agency, or recruiting directly, it is advisable to have a strategy for short-listing candidates. My favoured approach is to have a grid of essential and desired skills/experience and other factors and then spend time checking off candidates against the grid. By using a points system, it is easy to work out your order of preference. Be careful not to read too much into CVs! Many times a poorly worded CV does poor justice to a terrific candidate. I suggest that when advertising a vacancy directly or via an agency, you clarify any specific attributes, experience or skills that are crucial to the role and then expressly request that these are highlighted on a CV or application form.

Be flexible and prepared to read between the lines. I have often submitted candidates that have not 'jumped out' on paper but at interview have impressed me; only to have them recruited by my client despite the clients' initial scepticism. This neatly leads me onto the next point. If you have educated your agency to submit candidates on your behalf; then let them do their job! If they suggest you interview a candidate, then take their advice and do so. However, explain up front to your agency that if after 3 unsuitable candidates, you reserve the right to de-instruct the agency! I'm not suggesting that you say that you will hire 1 in 3, but if the agency submits 3 poorly matched candidates, sack or re-educate them.

The same approach goes for HR departments and recruiting managers. Work with them but explain exactly what you want. If your organisation is large enough to have 'in house recruiters' then let them do their job but explain how crucial it is that you identify suitable candidates within a specific time frame. If they can't come up with the right candidate within your deadline; then tell them you'll go 'outside'. Then watch how fast they can really move!

Application Forms

Many organisations use their own application forms; for a variety of reasons. It is a great way of ensuring that you have all the information YOU need, you get to see the applicants hand writing and you will often find out information NOT included in the CV. Be careful not to slip up with questions that get you into 'hot water'. For example, age is no longer deemed a question demanding a response in the EU and some states in the USA. Check with your HR advisor before you design your own one, or research and down load one from the web from an accredited source.

Arranging The Interview

Tempting, isn't it? You are the one with the job to offer! You are the one in control. Right? Well, maybe, but maybe not. Look, the reality is that with increased equality and the lack of exceptional candidates available, employers should at least consider that they might have to put themselves out to interview someone. Blasphemy to the 'old school' employers, but true none the less. If an applicant is in full time employment, then don't encourage them to 'take a sickie'. Nor should they have to sacrifice a half days work to attend an interview unless absolutely necessary. If using an agency or communicating with candidates directly, then discover what suits both parties best. Flexibility at this stage is fantastic for good will and if you genuinely do want to recruit THE BEST then this flexible approach will go a long way towards promoting a positive attitude towards future staff.

I know of one (real) estate agency firm who persists in making life difficult for potential employees; insisting that applicants attend interviews during office hours on prescribed days that suit them. The employer does this, I am convinced, out of some out dated view that they are the employer and demand some kind of Victorian 'respect'. The result? They struggle to hire exceptional candidates.

Pre Interview Communication

Following on from the previous paragraph, I strongly suggest that employers communicate with prospective employees quickly, effectively and elegantly. Elegantly you ask? Yes, elegantly! When arranging an interview, confirm dates/times in writing/email and include details about what the interview structure will be, the number of interviews, any assessments to be carried out on the day, proof of qualifications to be provided, background about the company etc etc etc (you get the idea).

The alternative is that you are slow to communicate, or do it poorly. This will be seen as a negative by many prospective employees. Remember, you need to 'sell' your opportunity, irrespective of economic circumstances.

If you are turning someone down, do it politely and quickly. You never know who the recipient may know! Your existing or potential biggest client! Just take care with communication as it is all part of your brand image. Great work done in the community or Social Media can often be destroyed by a poorly written refusal letter.

Chapter Eight

The Interview Process

This is not a book about interviewing technique itself. There are currently over 12,000 books with the word 'Interview' in the title on Amazon alone (other book sellers are available!) and if you take into account web based resources and DVDs/in house trainers, the resources available are phenomenal. I would urge the employing manager/owner/Director to consider that developing their skill as an interviewer is as important as management skills. I could argue that it is actually the MORE important skill as hiring the RIGHT person should reduce your management time in practice! I digress; of the many books about interviewing, I can recommend these:-

- Winning The Talent Wars by Bruce Tulgan

- Recruiting Excellence by Geoff Grout

- Winning by Jack & Suzy Welch

As far as the interview process itself (as opposed to technique) is concerned there are many things to consider:-

- Where will the interview take place

- How long should the interview last

- How many interviews will take place in your hiring process

- Will you interview individuals on their own or adopt an 'assessment' day format for a small group

- Consider 'taster' open evenings or weekends when attracting large numbers of applicants

- Will the 'style' be relaxed or more formal

- How many people will be involved in the process

- Will you ask competency based questions or will you request a practical assessment

- How will you decide who is the successful candidate

- Will you send out application forms in advance

- Will you take up references in advance or after the interview

- Will you send out any 'welcome' literature in advance

- How quickly will you inform the candidates of your decision

As far as the interview itself is concerned; these are my 'top tips' for success:-

- Know who you are due to interview; re-read their CV

- Prepare your interview questions

- Take notes

- Ensure that you are not disturbed

- Turn off your mobile phone, close your email account and re-divert your direct telephone number

- Use an 'ice breaker' to put the candidate at ease

- Advise colleagues that you are not to be interrupted

- Offer water and the option of using the 'facilities' before the interview

- Explain the selection process including timeframes

- Explain how long the interview will take

- Advise your role in the selection process and that of others

- Do not over-run

- Do not try to be funny or too informal

- Do not discuss politics, religion or football!

- Provide the opportunity for the removal of jackets in warm weather

- After asking a question; listen to the answer and do not interrupt

- Escort the candidate off the premises after the interview
- Always write with bad news as soon as possible
- Smile and be (relatively) nice!

Chapter Nine

Skills Testing and Personality Profiling

Over the last twenty five years or thereabouts, I have had the privilege of meeting many managers, directors and business owners. Intelligent, hard working people who want the best for their organisation. And yet many of these people continually fail to recruit the right person for the right job! In fact the money, time and resource I have seen wasted over the years has horrified me! The reason is that these employers refuse to employ a basic principal.

"Don't take their word for it!"

I encourage, urge and implore you to test your future employee's skills and abilities so that you can obtain an excellent appreciation of their ability to be effective in the role in question.

In reality, the candidate who succeeds in being offered the job is rarely the best choice, with the most suitable skills. He DID interview better however, and because the employer 'liked' him, he was hired; even though he could not spell or use a spread-sheet!

Suppose you manage a football team about to play a vital match and your goal keeper is injured. You would not draft in a replacement without asking him to train with the squad! Would you hire a bricklayer for your construction team without asking him to show you a brick wall he'd built or even lay a couple of courses of bricks in front of you as a demonstration? Of course not!

And yet, so few employers put their candidates through any kind of assessment at all. True, it's not always possible to assess a trainee's ability; however at the very least set some numeracy, literacy and IT skills tests. Recruitment agencies should do this as a matter of course and provide you with the results. How fast can they REALLY type, how good is their geographical spelling, is their German really commercial or is it simply conversational? Find out, I urge you!

With the abundance of on line IT testing facilities available, there is no excuse for not understanding exactly how accurate an applicant's data entry is or how proficient they are at using Excel, Word or a web design package.

For sales people, it is a little more complex. But by asking how the candidate would deal with specific objections or organise their day, you will get a reasonable understanding of their abilities. I have many clients who, at my suggestion, request that the potential candidate(s) spend a (half) day at the organisation actually shadowing the current employee or carrying out the duties. Trainee sales people should spend a day or two 'in the field' to see if they actually like the role and for the employer to observe them in 'action'. Do they have the 'spirit'? For experienced sales staff, it might be appropriate to actually shadow them in the field for a day or two. Yes, it can be time consuming. But consider the time wasted if you hire the wrong candidate and have to replace him!

Additionally, I am a strong advocate of psychometric testing in it's many different forms. Again, this book is not designed to be an exhaustive assessment of the pros and cons of the different systems, however, I can say that my staff and I have found it to be a very effective tool in understanding just what makes people 'tick'. I would not propose that such profiling tools should be the basis upon which you make your decision, however as part of the decision making process, I consider that the practice of profiling candidates has significant merit.

Psychometric profiling helps the employer understand exactly how the candidate will behave and if they are appropriate for a particular role. No one wants to hire an accountant who is sloppy and struggles with detail! How about hiring a sales person who struggles with rejection or a customer service person who is unable to build empathy? Likewise, most profiling systems will illustrate how the candidate will behave under pressure. More complex (and expensive) assessments will suggest suitable career options and propose interview questions. Others will carry out management audits, highlighting strengths and potential staff management issues. Useful? Essential, I believe, and a real resource in the hiring manager's 'tool kit'.

Ideally, I suggest that a business owner invest the time to become proficient at carrying out such assessments himself. As an alternative, engage the services of an HR consultant to carry out such assessments and explain the results to you or if using a recruitment firm, make sure that they use a recognised profiling tool and that the recruiter/consultant is qualified and understands how to interpret the findings.

Using such management tools can save an organisation thousands of pounds against the cost of recruiting the 'wrong' person.

Chapter Ten

Making the Offer

You would think that this would be simple! You interview a red-hot candidate, and you offer them the role. They either accept or refuse, right? Well, this might be the logical approach, however in any economic climate exceptional candidates are likely to have been on more than one interview and are, indeed, likely to have more than one offer in the pipeline.

Whatever the economic climate, great people are highly sought after. Whatever the economy; whatever the salary or role my strong advice is that you do not prevaricate! Take action and take it fast. Pick up the phone and make contact, either directly or via the agency and then follow it up with a letter and contract of employment. If you are not able to issue the contact of employment immediately then at least make the call and send out the offer letter as soon as you can. Occasionally, I have heard of organisations requesting a letter by return from the future employee as confirmation BEFORE the contract is issued. I can see the point of course; get some form of commitment before you spend time and effort sending off a contact. On balance, however I believe that it's better to send the contact with a request that your new employee has received it and will be starting on a specific date. If no confirmation is forthcoming; look for the alarm bells! I'd be on the phone really fast to establish whether they are still joining.

Also, how do you ensure that you are paying the candidate the right money and are not at risk of them accepting a better offer later? Do your research properly or if using a recruitment organisation, ask them to bench-mark for you. Get them to provide comparables of other vacancies that they have successfully filled that are similar to yours. If conducting your own research, look at local papers and job websites. If it is a specialist role, look at trade magazines or call your trade association for advice. You've paid your membership after all!

Be prepared to pay for it! Imagine that you are looking for an administrator and the going rate is, say £18,000. You interview a fantastic candidate who was earning £17,000 and has just been made redundant from her current company where she had worked for five years. This is obviously a steady, loyal character who probably knew that she was earning below market rate but chose to stay there for any number of reasons that could have included location, work colleagues etc. Now she's on the open market. You may well offer £16,000 or even £17,000 and think that you've 'got a bargain'. The trouble is that at this stage she has no loyalty to you. There is a fair chance that she knows what she's worth but will take your offer to ensure that she can pay her bills. But guess what? She's still keeping her eyes open and if someone else offers her the going rate, £18,000, she'll be off! Don't think you're being clever by offering less than the job is worth as there is a very good chance that it will cost you more in the long run. Imagine the scene; six months after your new secretary has joined, she resigns because she has accepted another position at £2,000 more! "Well then I'll offer her more money" you say. Too late I'm afraid.....she's going to a company that respects its staff enough to pay the market rate. Additionally you face the daunting prospect of commencing another campaign to replace her; with the associated costs and time demands. Don't end up being someone else's training resource!

Chapter Eleven

Contracts of Employment

When I first started work back in the early 1980's, all one invariably received from a new employer was a basic offer of employment confirming salary and start dates along with an employees' handbook that laid down a few basic roles and regulations. How things have changed over the last thirty years! If anyone is still of the opinion that they, as the employer, have 'the upper hand', then they are quite wrong! Employment law and employee rights have evolved dramatically, especially since the introduction of European regulation.

Whilst I believe that balance needed to be introduced, employment law is now, in my humble opinion, biased too far in the favour of the employee. Ask any modern Human Resources Manager how difficult it is to oust an under-performing employee and they will tell you stories that will make your toes curl. Employers who are taken to Employment Tribunal will often find, in my view, that the law is stacked against them.

This subject warrants not only a mighty tome of its own but is also one that demands regular review. I would strongly urge *any* employer to engage the services of a specialist employment lawyer to review, update or completely rewrite your letter of employment, contract of employment, employees' hand book and grievance and disciplinary procedures. Alternatively there are specialist HR consultants who are qualified to provide such a service. I would, with the greatest of respect to general practice solicitors, suggest that you ensure that this work is conducted by a professional who specialises in this work. This particular area of law is changing so fast that unless the professional in question specialises, they probably won't be fully up to date. Many larger law firms now have specialist employment law departments in the way that they have family law, commercial, criminal, probate and conveyancing departments.

Just to give you a flavour of the areas that need to be covered in a modern contract of employment consider the following issues, for example:-

- Paternity rights. Just how much leave is a new father permitted during the first year after his child has been born, and at what % of full pay?

- The length of the working week. Employees can work no more than 48 hours on average over a 17 week period.

- Privacy policy. Do you advise your staff that you have the right to monitor their emails?

- Internet policy. Do you clarify whether you permit your staff to surf the internet, for what purposes and for how long? Do you restrict the sites they may visit; excluding, for example, those of an 'adult nature'?

- What are your procedures for dealing with under -performing staff? You can't simply kick someone out these days! Your process must be declared in advance.

- Competition and confidentiality. What do you have in place if a key member of staff (or sales person perhaps) moves to a competitor? Will it stand up in court?

The above is designed to help you realise that this is a huge subject; the law is changing daily and needs to be taken seriously. If you are interested in keeping abreast of the subject I can recommend Croners' publications.

My final recommendation on this sombre subject is that you take immediate action. Do not expect professional advice to come cheap...but expect it to cost you a lot less than the alternative!

Chapter Twelve

Post Offer Acceptance Strategy

Just because you have offered your 'dream candidate' a position with your organisation, don't think that it is a dead 'cert' that they will actually turn up on the appointed day! If there is a delay of anything more than a couple of days between the offer being made and the person's anticipated start date there is always the danger that they may accept a counter offer from their current employers or perhaps accept an offer from another organisation that has been made subsequent to yours.

You could be forgiven for thinking that there is little that you can do to avoid this unfortunate situation or even you become philosophical and believe that if they did not want to join you that they are 'not the right one anyway.' However the fact that you have invested a great deal of time and effort in short listing and subsequently offering this person employment means that you *were* pretty keen on them and as a result it would make sense to put in place a few simple procedures to secure your investment.

Whether you are recruiting via a recruitment organisation or completely as a result of your own efforts these following points will dramatically increase the chances of 'your' new employee turning up on day one:-

- With any contract of employment enclose a covering letter that warmly welcomes your new employee to your organisation. Request that they read and sign a copy of the contract of employment, to be returned to you before a specific date prior to the commencement of employment. If possible request that they contact you to arrange a time too pop in to the office so that they may physically hand over the document and discuss with you any areas requiring clarification.

- Send, with contract if possible any marketing literature or employees' hand-book. You should have already provided the candidate with a full job description, however there is no harm in sending another copy for their information.

- Arrange for your new starter to meet with their new manager or team members prior to the commencement date. The format could either be at a company social event or on a more formal basis during office hours.

- At the point of offer, rather than simply dropping a letter in the post, contact the candidate by phone and warmly make the offer. Enquire as to whether they have any other irons in the fire and how your offer 'matches up'. If the candidate does accept your offer make sure that they are genuinely interested and not just telling you what you want to hear.

- Contact your new member of staff every week before the appropriate start date. If there are problems or if they are having second thoughts your should be able to hear the uncertainty in their voice.

Chapter Thirteen

Protecting Your Investment

Protecting your 'investment' in the recruitment of your new staff is crucial. Why would you invest time in identifying, interviewing and recruiting new staff only to have another employer 'sneak in' and 'steal' your new recruit from under your nose. Falling at the 'final hurdle' is painful, yet can be so easily prevented with just a little planning. If you think that they are worth hiring, so will someone else. Additionally, because the new employee has not yet joined your company, they will not have formed any sense of loyalty or bond with any colleagues.

Be aware that other recruiters might still be trying to offer the individual other opportunities and additionally, previous employers might be inclined to make a counter offer.

It is impossible to avoid such situations but you can reduce the risk of 'your' new member of staff 'listening' to such offers. Keeping in contact between offer and start date is simple and highly effective. Send the new employee company literature and invite them to a social event. Issuing the company handbook in advance is an excellent idea. After issue, call and ask if there are any queries. Above all it's about communication.

As a side issue, I would urge employers NOT to make counter offers to employees. If they have resigned, there will be a number of reasons. Yes, more money or a promotion might change their minds; for now! Evidence shows that those who have resigned and subsequently been 'bought back' will leave within a year. Why? Because it is rarely 'just' about the money. The office is still too far away and they still don't find the role stimulating. Let them go! Yes, it will be inconvenient; but inconvenience today is better than resentment tomorrow when they resign again.

Chapter Fourteen

Commencement and Induction

My recruitment business recently carried out a survey. We discovered that 73% of all people had had no induction! Put yourself in the shoes of the new member of staff for a moment. The new employee is thrilled about starting their new job and of course they have been 'sold' the idea or myth of the role and then they have their dreams dashed by a lousy or non-existent induction course.

I suggest that you have a 'tick sheet' of all the aspects of an appropriate induction course. Don't be so keen to get your new member of staff at their desk or workstation. Spend time with them explaining the company's history, ethos, plans and culture. In our business, we describe our clients' profiles, our company structure, systems and processes. Every business has a unique DNA and whilst those who have been employed understand this, new comers are naïve and it is helpful to have an opportunity to 'download' this.

It is a really good idea to take the employee through the contract of employment and the employees' handbook, explaining unusual terminology. Consider reviewing matters at the end of first week and ask for any areas that need to be clarified or explained.

Above all don't allow a new employee to believe that they have been miss-sold the role, company or opportunity. Working hard on an induction course will pay dividends and can be adjusted and developed for other roles as times go by.

Chapter Fifteen

Retaining Talent

Let's be honest with each other for a moment shall we? Not everybody that you will hire will be vital to the growth of your organisation; some will come and go. However, what I have realised by studying organisations that have grown over the last 25 years is that they are always looking at their employees, trying to identify potential superstars. Future managers and directors often come from within your organisation. It is essential, therefore, that you are firstly aware of such talent and secondly that you nurture and develop it. My research tells me that whilst money is an important factor in the attraction and retention of staff; they actually stay for a wider number of factors, including the relationships with other staff and Directors. Job content, training opportunities and promotional prospects are also crucial to the retention of staff, as are staff social events, appraisals and recognition. Even critical feedback is often appreciated. How can a member of staff improve if they are only ever praised?

I consider the failure of most organisations to provide regular appraisals as one of the main reasons that staff feel disgruntled and leave. Likewise; appraisals, if properly and regularly conducted, can be an incredibly powerful, motivational tool for the development of staff. I have no intention of describing an appraisal system as I have used many different models over the years and have seen many others in operation with clients. There are many books written about appraisals by those with greater authority than me and a host of on line tools; however these are some of the ingredients of an effective appraisal system:-

- Should be held regularly, ideally monthly, if not quarterly or at the very least annually

- Plenty of notice should be provided to the employee

- The employee should have time to prepare their own comments/self appraisal in advance during office hours

- Any scheduled appraisals should take place on the allocated day and not re-arranged
- Appraisals should be confidential and held in private
- Notes should be taken
- Feedback should be constructive and not accusational
- Previous appraisal notes should be referred to
- 360 degree appraisals can be useful but may be difficult for some employers to deal with!

In a survey that I had commissioned in 2011/2012, I established the top 3 reasons that employees were looking to leave their current organisation:-

1. Money
2. Lack of opportunity to progress
3. Lack of training

Additionally, I established the top 3 reasons that employees remain with their employers.

1. Relationships with their colleagues
2. Job content
3. A great boss (yes, really!)

Naturally, the reasons that people leave and remain are often affected by the prevailing economic climate. However, I believe that these lists are rather illuminating. Whilst money is the main reason for leaving, it would appear that relationships rather than money are the main reasons for staying put! Long hours would appear not to feature very highly. These results are incredibly useful when understanding the reasons that people stay and what employers can put in place to help retain superstars. I would, however suggest that any employer carry out a confidential survey 'in house' as there were a number of anomalies and it would be negligent of me to suggest that the reasons stated above relate to YOUR organisation. In the pursuance of accurate information; I urge you to carry out your own research.

Accountants, for example, stay for very different reasons than sales staff.

For a copy of the Staff Survey, please email me:-

help@therecruitmentguy.com

Since 1988 I have observed some exceptional examples of 'best practice' with regards to staff retention. Those that really do mean "our best asset is our staff" back it up with lots of 'little' things that help people feel valued. This list is by no means exhaustive and is no particular order.

1. Limited and agreed access to the internet during break-times

2. Staff social events

3. Suggestion boxes

4. Clearly defined goals

5. Dress down 'Fridays'

6. Career advancement programmes

7. Early finish on Friday as a sign of recognition

8. Free tea & coffee

9. Being listened to

10. Brainstorming events

Conclusions

In this book I have tried to provide the reader with a 'tool box' of resources for owners and non-HR managers of businesses. If I have managed to convey how the 'best companies' really do strive to attract, develop and retain outstanding staff then my objective has been achieved. Whether you 'DIY' or engage a recruitment firm to assist you, the task of recruiting 'the right' staff is possible; it just needs some thought and planning.

The responsibility to assist a company by recruiting its staff is a true honour, whether you are an internal manager or a 'hired hand'. If this book inspires and further educates one company to hold itself to a higher standard, then it has accomplished my aims.

I am humbled that you read this far; thank you!

What They Say...

"Having engaged Graham Martin to recruit office juniors to finance and marketing managers for nearly 20 years I am fully aware that he knows what he's doing! His book guides business managers through the labyrinth of recruitment in easy to understand steps. A useful little book that makes so much sense."
Clive M Coote, MD, Vertical Leisure UK

"No book can ever solve all your recruitment problems – but this one is sure to help !"
Mike Franklin, Managing Director, Lanes New Homes, England

"As a US based recruiter of 25 years, I know good practices when I see them. For the newbie or experienced, Graham has it in spades; his book proves it!"
Diane Alper, Alper and Associates San Francisco

"This is a real 'hands-on' guide to the subject written by a true expert"
Norma Morris, Partner, Curwens Solicitors, England

Acknowledgements

Writing a book seemed a great idea at the time; but it took a lot longer than I had originally anticipated! Life got in the way! I'd like to thank those who encouraged me to finally finish and who believed in my ability, specifically my good friend and inspiration Gavin Ingham, my long suffering business partner Karen Leggett and my children Elliott and Phoebe. Thank you to all those who proof read and helped with suggestions. Lastly, I'd like to thank my Mum, Joyce Martin to whom I dedicate this book.

Graham Martin
Enfield, London
December 2012

I have also created a series of videos to assist employers recruit staff. You can find them at
www.therecruitmentguy.com/employers

You can contact me via
help@therecruitmentguy.com

For help in recruiting staff you can contact me at Orchard Recruitment in London
graham@orchardjobs.com
UK 020 8366 9014

The Author

Born and educated in Hertfordshire, Graham Martin's earlier careers were in banking in the City of London and estate agency residential sales in North London, before opening Orchard Recruitment in 1988. Now focusing on management and accountancy appointments, he has personally recruited nearly 1700 people on behalf of client companies, from a tea lady called Ivy to Finance Directors.

Under the guise of The Recruitment Guy, Graham has also presented to and led seminars with thousands of teenage and University students covering a variety of work and career-related issues, including CV writing, interview tips and work experience. Appearing on radio and with a website designed for school and college leavers, he is arguably one of the leading 'hands on' experts in his field.

Living in North London, Graham has two children and spends his spare time indulging in his three passions: classic cars, gardening and sailing.

This is his first book for employers and is a distillation of 25 years of experience at the 'sharp end' of recruitment.